MINIBEASTS UP CLOSE

Ants
Up Close

Robin Birch

Raintree

www.raintreepublishers.co.uk
Visit our website to find out more information about **Raintree** books.

To order:
 Phone 44 (0) 1865 888112
Send a fax to 44 (0) 1865 314091
Visit the Raintree Bookshop at **www.raintreepublishers.co.uk** to browse our catalogue and order online.

Published in 2004 by Heinemann Library
a division of Harcourt Education Australia,
18–22 Salmon Street, Port Melbourne Victoria 3207 Australia
(a division of Reed International Books Australia Pty Ltd,
ABN 70 001 002 357).
Visit the Heinemann Library website @
www.heinemannlibrary.com.au

First published in Great Britain by Raintree,
Halley Court, Jordan Hill, Oxford OX2 8EJ,
part of Harcourt Education.
Raintree is a registered trademark of Harcourt Education Ltd.

A Reed Elsevier company

Editorial: Carmel Heron, Anne McKenna
Design: Stella Vassiliou, Marta White
Photo research: Jes Senbergs, Wendy Duncan
Illustration: Rob Mancini
Production: Tracey Jarrett

Typeset in Officina Sans 19/23 pt
Pre-press by Digital Imaging Group (DIG)
Printed in China by WKT Company Ltd.

The paper used to print this book comes from sustainable resources.

National Library of Australia Cataloguing-in-Publication data:

Birch, Robin.
    Ants up close.

    Includes index.
    For primary students.
    ISBN 1 74070 189 5.

    1. Ants - Juvenile literature. I. Title. (Series : Birch,
    Robin. Minibeasts up close).

595.796

Acknowledgements

The publisher would like to thank the following for permission
to reproduce photographs: ANT Photo Library/Jan Taylor: p. **10**,
/Densey Clyne: p. **27**; APL-Minden/© Mark Moffatt: p. **22**;
Auscape/Greg Harold: pp. **14, 15**, /Kathie Atkinson: p. **19**;
Bruce Coleman Inc/Kim Taylor: p. **8**; Corbis/George B. Diebold:
p. **16**; Great Southern Stock/Denis Crawford: p. **13**; Lochman
Transparencies/Jiri Lochman: pp. **6, 7, 12**; © The Natural History
Museum, London: pp. **20, 28**; Nature Picture Library: p. **25**;
OSF/Konrad Wothe: p. **5**; photolibrary.com: p. **17**,
photolibrary.com/Science Photo Library/William Ervin: p. **23**,
/Pascal Goetgheluck: p. **29**, /Susumu Nishinaga: p. **11**,
/Sinclair Stammers: p. **4**; © Queensland Museum/Jeff Wright:
pp. **18, 26**; Texas A & M University/ C. L. Barr: p. **24**.

Cover photograph of a bulldog ant worker on leaf reproduced
with permission of ANT Photo Library/Chris & Sandra Pollitt.

Every attempt has been made to trace and acknowledge
copyright. Where an attempt has been unsuccessful, the
publisher would be pleased to hear from the copyright owner
so any omission or error can be rectified.

Contents

Any words appearing in bold, **like this**, are explained in the Glossary.

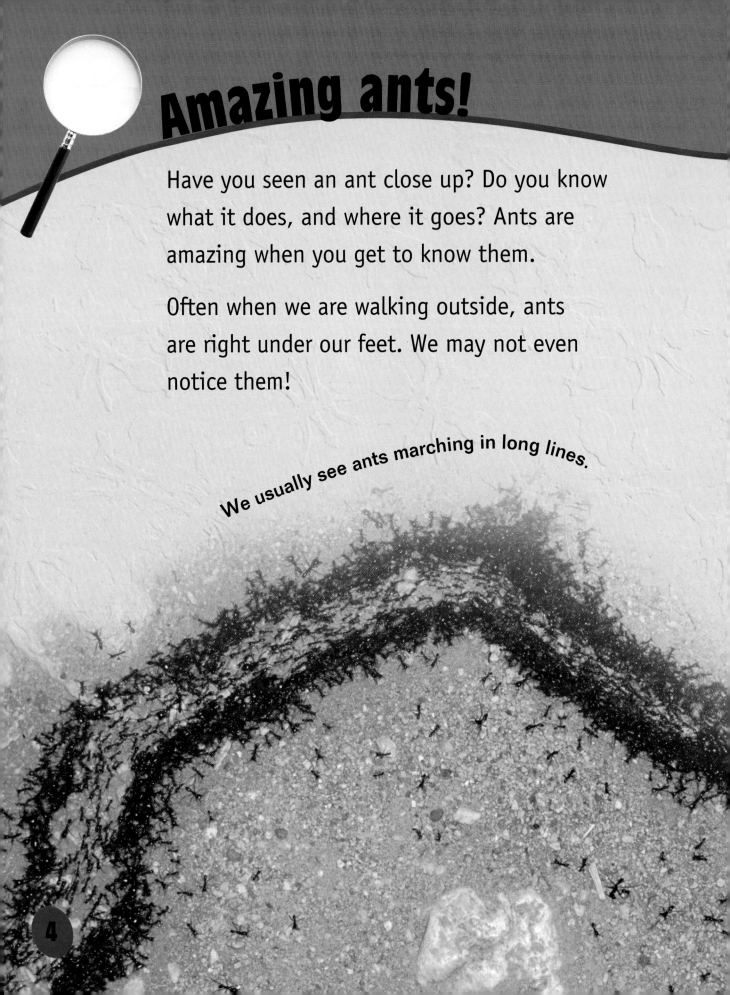

Amazing ants!

Have you seen an ant close up? Do you know what it does, and where it goes? Ants are amazing when you get to know them.

Often when we are walking outside, ants are right under our feet. We may not even notice them!

We usually see ants marching in long lines.

What are ants?

Ants are insects. Insects are animals that have six legs. They also have a thin, hard skin called an **exoskeleton** on the outside of the body, instead of bones inside the body.

There are more than 15,000 kinds, or **species**, of ants in the world. The largest ants are as long as a pen lid (4 centimetres), while some are about the size of a grain of sand (less than 1 millimetre).

Ants can carry things 50 times heavier than they are. This is like a person carrying a bulldozer!

Where do ants live?

Ants live in most parts of the world. More ants live in warm places than in cold places. Ants live in forests, open areas, and in deserts. They live wherever they can find food.

Ants live in groups called **colonies**. Most ant colonies live in underground nests.

Nests

Most kinds of ants make nests to live in. They usually make them in the soil. While ants are under ground in a nest, they are living in darkness. They come up above ground to look for their food.

Some ants live in trees. They do not usually come down to the ground. These ants are often found in hot, wet parts of the world.

Army ants

Army ants are different from other ants – they do not make nests. Instead, they move about in long wide lines, like an army marching. They carry their eggs and young ants with them.

Some ants make nests of leaves, in trees.

7

Ant body parts

An ant's body has three parts. First is
the head, then the **thorax** in the middle and
then the **abdomen** (ab-da-men) at the end.

The head

The head has feelers called **antennae** (an-ten-ay)
on it, as well as eyes and mouthparts.

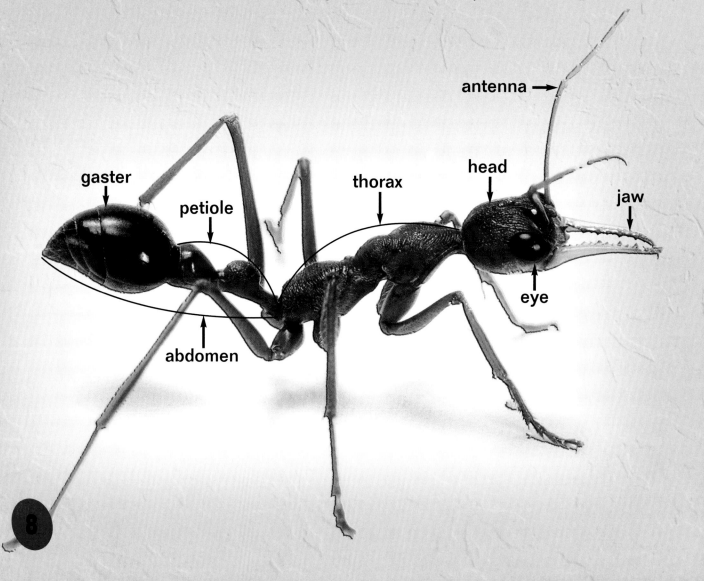

antenna ➡

gaster

thorax

head

jaw

petiole

eye

abdomen

The thorax

The thorax has six legs joined to it. Some ants have wings attached to the thorax.

The abdomen

The abdomen has two parts. The first part is called the **petiole** (<u>pet</u>-ee-ole). It is very narrow, and makes a small waist. Then the abdomen becomes wider and rounder. This part is called the gaster. Some ants have a sting on the end of the abdomen.

The exoskeleton

An ant's **exoskeleton** covers the whole of its body. It gives the ant its shape and protects the ant from being hurt easily. It also stops the ant from drying out by trapping water inside its body.

Mouthparts and eating

Most ants eat food from plants. They eat seeds, and **liquids** such as **nectar** and **sap**.

Some ants are hunters. They catch small animals such as insects, spiders and centipedes.

Jaws

An ant's mouth has two strong **jaws**, which open out sideways. The jaws usually have pointed teeth. Ants carry, cut and crush food with their jaws. Some ants can bite animals with them.

Ants have biting mouthparts.

Eating

An ant has four small **palps**, like fingers, near its mouth. An ant can move its food to its mouth with its palps.

An ant has a tongue below its mouth. As the ant laps up food with its tongue, pieces that cannot be swallowed collect in a pocket between the tongue and the mouth. When the pocket is full, the ant empties it onto the nest's rubbish heap.

An ant chooses food by touching and tasting it with its palps.

palp ⟶

Eyes and seeing

Most ants have two large eyes. Each eye is made of up to 1000 smaller eyes. This kind of eye is called a **compound** eye.

Flying ants have three tiny eyes on the top of their head. Scientists think these eyes probably only see light and dark, and that they may help the ants to fly.

Ants' eyes are on the side of their head.

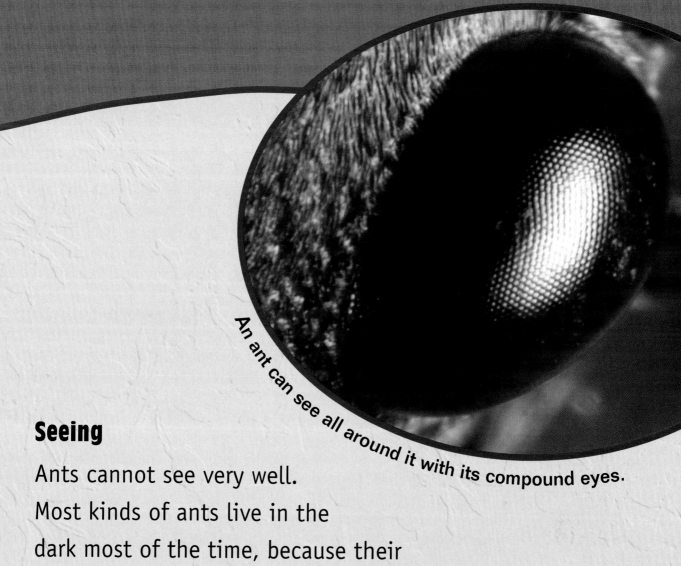

An ant can see all around it with its compound eyes.

Seeing

Ants cannot see very well. Most kinds of ants live in the dark most of the time, because their nests are under ground. Some ants have no eyes at all. These ants may live under ground all the time.

Some ants can see where the sun is, when they are out looking for food. They use the sun as a guide, to see which direction to go in.

Finding their way

Red harvester ants gather seeds far away from their nests. They find their way back to their nests by looking at large objects such as trees and bushes, and using them as signposts.

13

Antennae and sensing

An ant has two long feelers called **antennae** on the front of its head. It smells and touches food and other ants with them. It also uses its antennae to follow smell trails left behind by other ants.

An ant can hear sounds and feel **vibrations** in the ground with its antennae.

The antennae have a bend in them. The ant can fold them back over its head when there is danger, so they are not damaged.

Tasting

An ant tastes with its mouthparts. It tastes its food, and it tastes other ants when it licks them.

Hairs

An ant has hairs all over its body. The hairs are closest together on the legs and feelers. These hairs help the ant **sense** when there are other things around it.

Ants have short hairs on most parts of their exoskeleton. Some ants have **spines** as well.

Legs for moving

Ants have six legs, three on each side of the **thorax**. Each leg has three main parts, and a long foot.

Walking

Ants can walk easily over rough ground. They can hold on when they walk up walls or trees, and walk upside down.

When ants walk or run, they move the front and back leg on one side forward at the same time as the middle leg on the other side. This helps them move easily.

Ants' feet have two curved claws on the end of them, for gripping and holding.

Useful legs

Ants use their front legs to hold food and to hold their young when they are feeding them.

Jumper ants

Jumper ants are black and yellow. If their nests are disturbed, several will attack in short jumping movements.

Ants can lift their legs and rub them over their whole body, to clean themselves.

17

The **thorax** is the middle part of the ant's body, and the **abdomen** is the end part.

The thorax

The thorax has six legs joined to it. Male ants and young queen ants have two pairs of wings joined to the thorax. Some ants have two **spines** on the back end of the thorax.

The abdomen

The front part of the abdomen is called the **petiole**. It is small and has one or two sections.

petiole

Unlike some other insects, ants have a 'waist', called the petiole, between their thorax and abdomen.

Ants can bring the abdomen under the thorax, until the end of the abdomen reaches the mouth. In this way, a stinging ant can bite, and use its sting to poison the victim at the same time.

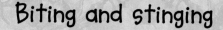

An ant's sting is on the end of its abdomen.

Stings

Some ants have a sting on the end of their abdomen. They use the sting to catch their **prey** and to protect themselves.

The sting is a pointed tube that the ant sticks into its victim. A stinging poison comes out of the tube and goes into the victim.

Some kinds of ants have a sting that sprays the poison onto the victim.

Inside an ant

An ant's heart is long and thin. It runs down the middle of the **thorax** and **abdomen**. The heart pumps blood around the body.

How does an ant get air?

Ants have three tiny air holes down each side of their thorax, and seven down each side of the abdomen. Ants take in air through these holes, called **spiracles** (<u>spi</u>-ra-kels). Tiny tubes then carry the air around the ant's body.

A close-up photograph of a spiracle.

What happens to food?

When ants collect food from outside the nest, they store it in their storage stomach. They pass it on to ants inside the nest by bringing it back out of their mouths. These ants may then feed it to other ants in the nest.

Some of the ant's food passes on to the food stomach, where it is **digested**. Waste parts of food pass out of the **anus** as droppings.

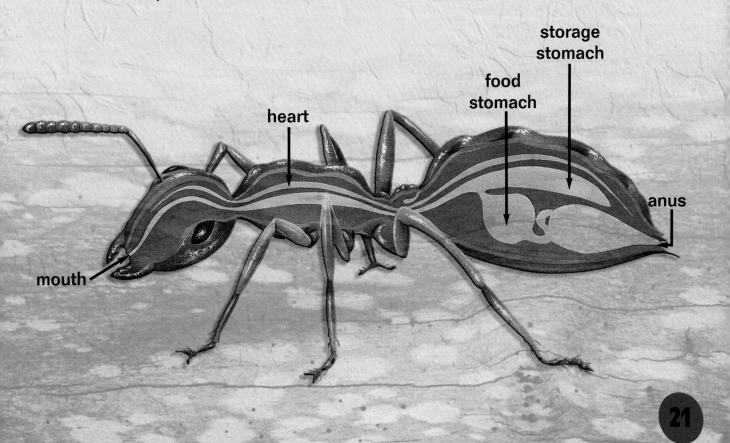

storage
stomach

food
stomach

heart

anus

mouth

21

An ant colony

Most ants live in a large group called a **colony**. Most colonies have queen ants, male ants and worker ants.

Queen ants

An ant colony has one or more queen ants. These female ants lay the eggs for the colony. They have wings when young. The queen ants are often much larger than the other ants, and may live for up to 15 years.

Most colonies build a nest to live in.

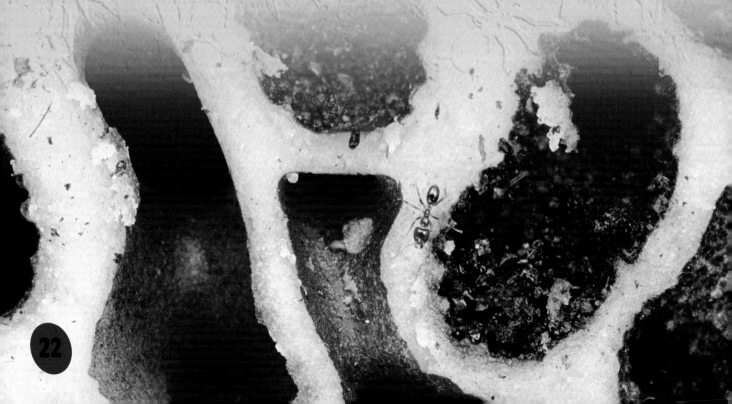

Male ants

Male ants also have wings, but often only live for a few days after becoming adults. They **mate** with a queen ant. They do not find their own food, but are fed by the worker ants.

Soldier ants

Some worker ants are larger than the others, and have big heads and **jaws**. These ants may use their big jaws for fighting, or crushing seeds. They are sometimes called soldier ants.

Worker ants

Worker ants are females. They do not have wings. Worker ants find food for the colony. They also look after the queen, the young and the nest. Usually they live for a few weeks or months.

Most of the ants we see are worker ants.

Life cycle of ants

While a queen ant is still young she finds a male, and they **mate**. The male ant dies soon after.

The queen then bites her wings off, or rubs them off against a rock. She no longer needs them, as she will live inside her nest for the rest of her life.

Most **species** of ants mate while they are flying.

Making a nest

After mating, the queen may make her nest by finding or digging a hole in the ground. She lays her first eggs. The worker ants that hatch out look after her, and she lays more eggs. The **colony** grows as more ants hatch.

Some kinds of queen ants do not make their own nests. Instead, they move back into their old nest, or another nest that already has many ants in it. These colonies can have several queen ants in them, all laying eggs for the colony.

After she has mated, a queen ant lays eggs in a hole in the ground.

Young ants

Ant eggs are white or light yellow. They are smaller than a speck of dust. The eggs hatch a few weeks after being laid. The hatched ants, called **larvae**, are grubs with no legs.

The larvae are given **liquid** food by worker ants. They grow until they are about as big as adult ants.

The worker ants feed and look after the larvae.

larvae

Becoming an adult

The larvae then stop moving and eating. They are now called **pupae**. While ants are pupae, they change from larvae into adult ants. Then they lose their skin.

A young adult ant is a light colour at first. It is fed for a while by worker ants, until it is ready to feed itself.

Cocoons

In some species, the larvae spin a **cocoon** for themselves before they become pupae. When they have become adults, worker ants open the cocoon for them.

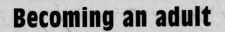

Ants and us

Have you ever left food out in your house and found it covered in ants? Ants go into our houses looking for something to eat.

Ants like sweet things and they also look for grains, fat or meat. Sometimes they are looking for water.

When lots of ants come into the house, they can be a nuisance.

We may not always notice ants, but they are always doing something interesting.

Carpenter ants

Carpenter ants make their nests in wood, by chewing holes in it. They can be pests to humans because they weaken wood in buildings.

Useful ants

Ants can clean up houses! Sometimes when people living in villages in Africa see lots of driver ants marching towards them, they leave their homes for a while so the ants can clean out pests. Driver ants can kill animals such as cockroaches, snakes, mice and scorpions. Many animals run away as the ants get near.

Find out for yourself

You may be able to find some ants outdoors. Look for a trail of ants, and see where they go. Can you find the entrance to their nest? Are the ants carrying food, such as seeds?

Books to read

Looking at Minibeasts: Ants, Bees and Wasps, Sally Morgan (Belitha Press, 2001)

Life in a Colony: Ants, Richard and Louise Spilbury (Heinemann Library, 2003)

Using the Internet

Explore the Internet to find out more about ants. Websites can change, so do not worry if the links below no longer work. Use a search engine, such as www.yahooligans.com or www.internet4kids.com, and type in a keyword such as 'ants', or the name of a particular ant.

Websites

www.enchantedlearning.com/subjects/insects/ants This site has activities, printouts and information about ants' body parts, colonies and life cycles.

www.antcam.com This site has two live cameras so you can see, as well as learn about, ants.

Disclaimer
All the Internet addresses (URLs) given in this book were valid at the time of going to press. However, due to the dynamic nature of the Internet, some addresses may have changed or ceased to exist since publication. While the author and publisher regret any inconvenience this may cause readers, no responsibility for any such changes can be accepted by either the author or the publisher.

Glossary

abdomen last of the three main sections of an insect

anus hole in the abdomen through which droppings are passed

antenna (plural: antennae) feeler on an insect's head

cocoon container or covering of silk

colony group of many insects of the same kind living together

compound made of smaller parts

digest break down food so an animal can use it for energy and growth

exoskeleton hard outside skin of an insect

jaw hard mouthpart that moves and often has teeth on it, usually used for biting and holding food

larva (plural: larvae) young stage of many insects, a grub

liquid something that is runny, not hard, such as juice

mate when a male and a female come together to produce young

nectar sweet juice from flowers

palp small body part like a finger, near an insect's mouth

petiole small first section of an ant's abdomen, which joins to the thorax

prey animal that is caught and eaten by another animal

pupa (plural: pupae) stage of an insect's life, when it changes from a larva to an adult

sap juice inside a plant

sense how an animal knows what is going on around it

species type or kind of animal; animals of the same species can produce young together

spine hard, pointed spike

spiracle tiny air hole on an insect's body

thorax chest part of an insect

vibration fast shaking movement

31

Index